THE UNITED METHODIST WAY

A Brief Overview of the
History, Beliefs, Mission, and Organization
Of The United Methodist Church

BRANSON L. THURSTON

DISCIPLESHIP RESOURCES

P.O. BOX 340003 • NASHVILLE, TN 37203-0003
www.discipleshipresources.org

This booklet is dedicated with love to my daughter, Blythe Lorraine (Lori) Thurston Smith, whose growth in discipleship has paralleled the life of this book. Special thanks are also due to my wife, Betty, and my son, Blake.

Reprinted 1998, 2000, 2004

ISBN 0-88177-215-1

DR215

THE UNITED
METHODIST WAY

Our decision to become members of The United Methodist Church is more than a promise to take part in special programs at a special building called "church."

It is more like committing ourselves to a life-long voyage on a great sailing ship—

—a ship that has been given the mission of rescuing persons:

Persons struggling to stay afloat upon tossing waves;

Persons starving upon isolated and lonely islands.

The purpose of this booklet is to help you . . .

Learn where the ship has come from (see "History," p. 3);

Explore the major theological understandings that support and direct our voyage (see "Beliefs," p. 17);

Learn more about the ship's sailing orders, its reason for being (see "Mission," p. 24);

Review the structure of the ship that enables it to fulfill its mission (see "Organization," p. 35).

Of course, this little booklet is just a beginning. As you become interested in each of these areas, plan to do further reading. You may wish to secure some of the resources listed on pages 45-46. Perhaps you'll want to speak to your pastor about organizing a small group to explore some of these concerns more fully.

You are invited to use *The United Methodist Way* as a springboard into a lifelong adventure in learning about our church, helping to direct its mission, and joining in its ministries with all people.

HISTORY

Our ship — The United Methodist Church — was launched in 1968. But it was fashioned from the timbers, masts, and sails of two seasoned ships that had already been sailing upon the seas. Those two earlier vessels were The Methodist Church and The Evangelical United Brethren Church, which had separate ports of origin.

The Evangelical United Brethren Church reflected the 1946 uniting of . . .

The Evangelical Church, and
The Church of the United Brethren in
    Christ.

The Methodist Church reflected the 1939 reuniting of . . .

The Methodist Protestant Church,
The Methodist Episcopal Church, and
The Methodist Episcopal Church, South.

These three denominations had split in the nineteenth century over the issues of slavery and the involvement of lay persons in making major church decisions.

Our Methodist Heritage

The three Methodist bodies that were re-united in 1939 shared a memory and a heritage that included . . .

John Wesley, the founder of Methodism in England, and other early leaders of a revival movement that eventually became a church;

The Christmas Conference of 1784 at which The Methodist Episcopal Church was established in the New World.

John Wesley (1703-1791) and his younger brother Charles (1707-1788) were two of nineteen children born to Samuel and Susanna Wesley. Samuel was a clergyman who served the Epworth parish north of London.

Both Samuel and Susanna began each child's education when he or she reached the age of five; the training was thorough and demanding. Susanna also set aside one hour each week with each child to discuss religious concerns. It was not by accident that John Wesley would later seek Susanna's judgment before he made decisions that would change the religious life of England and America.

Through Samuel's efforts and Susanna's training, John and Charles both entered Oxford University. There John also became an instructor. In the meantime, Charles founded a group at Oxford—the Holy Club—and asked John to serve as its leader. The club originally met to discuss the classics, but it soon came to focus its attention on religious concerns at a time when religion was not taken too seriously. Members led such disciplined, methodical lives of worship, study, and service that fellow students laughingly called them "Methodists." The name was to stick, first to the movement, and then to the denomination.

Despite his ordination as a minister in the Church of England, and his active and disciplined religious life, John Wesley remained unsatisfied. At a crucial point he met a group of Moravians who helped him identify what he was seeking: The concrete assurance of God's love, and vitality in the Christian life.

That assurance and vitality came into focus on May 24, 1738, as Wesley met with a society gathered on Aldersgate Street in London. As someone read Luther's description of the change God works in our hearts, Wesley felt his own heart "strangely warmed." He knew then that he did indeed trust Christ and Christ alone for his salvation.

Tirelessly, the Wesley brothers organized groups in which persons could support and strengthen one another in Christian faith and life. In town after town, members of the Methodist "society" would gather for preaching services and earnest sharing. In turn, each society was divided into "classes" of about twelve members, intimate groups that met weekly for self-examination, Bible study, and prayer.

Influenced and encouraged by George Whitefield, John Wesley recognized that the message must be preached in fields and streets to people who had no intention of stepping inside a church. Soon Wesley established a corps of lay preachers who proclaimed the good news of God's love wherever people were to be found. The lay preachers also came to America, and the societies took root there as well.

American Methodist Roots

The first Methodist society in New York City was born largely through the efforts of Barbara Heck. She and her family came from Ireland to New York in 1760.

Her cousin, Philip Embury, had been a local preacher with the Methodist societies in Ireland, but in New York his energies were absorbed in finding work and establishing his trade as a carpenter. When Barbara Heck found her brother and others involved in a gambling card game, she threw the cards into the fire. Rushing to Embury's house, she urged her cousin to preach and establish a society. With Heck's prodding and encouragement the society was established in Embury's house. It rapidly outgrew those quarters and rented a room near the barracks.

During one of the meetings a British officer entered the room, introducing himself as "Captain Thomas Webb, of the King's service, and also a soldier of the cross and a spiritual son of John Wesley." Under the leadership of Heck, Embury, and Webb, the society prospered and became John Street Church in New York City.

With the Revolution many of the American clergy of the established English church returned home. Citizens of the new country wanted to maintain a vital church life that included participation in the sacraments of Baptism and the Lord's Supper, yet only clergy could administer the sacraments. Wesley saw that new steps had to be taken.

After much thought and prayer, Wesley consecrated Thomas Coke as a "general superintendent" to go to America. There Coke was to ordain Wesley's lay preachers and to make Frances Asbury a superintendent. A conference for this purpose was called for Christmas Eve 1784, at Lovely Lane Chapel in Baltimore.

With this Christmas Conference the Methodist movement in America became an organized church. Asbury, reflecting the democratic spirit of the new land, would agree to be a superintendent only if elected by his fellow ministers. This they quickly did. Within a few years the title of "general superintendent" was changed to "bishop."

As a bishop, Asbury traveled over 275,000 miles — on horseback and on foot from New York to Tennessee, preaching and supervising the work of the new church.

The influence of John Wesley is still apparent in our United Methodist organization—which is *episcopal* (bishops serve as general superintendents) and *connectional* (congregations are related to one another through regional and national structures).

And we have inherited many of Wesley's spiritual emphases:

A faith that is both informed and warmly experienced;

A religion that is intensely personal but must be shared with others;

A concern for the spiritual, physical, and social conditions of all persons;

An affirmation of belief in one God as revealed through Jesus Christ—but an appreciation for a variety of ways in which that affirmation may be expressed.

Charles Wesley's influence also continues — not only through the ways in which he helped John — but also through his hymns. He wrote over 6,000 hymns, many of which continue to be sung by Christians throughout the world. To list but a few:

"O for a thousand tongues to sing"
"Love divine, all loves excelling"
"Hark! The herald angels sing"
"Christ the Lord is risen today"
"Rejoice, the Lord is King"
"A charge to keep I have"
"I want a principle within"

As for George Whitefield, he and John Wesley had a strong disagreement over the doctrine of predestination, which Wesley rejected but which Whitefield came to accept. As intense as their argument was, both men recognized an even greater unity they shared in Christ. Within the sermons of both Wesley and Whitefield can be found affirmations that our kinship in Christ and the central core of beliefs shared by Christians through the ages are more important than our individual theological differences.

Our EUB Heritage

When The United Methodist Church was formed in 1968, The Evangelical United Brethren (EUB) Church brought to the union . . .

A kindred spirit with the Methodists that could be traced back to early days in America;

Its own previous merger of The Evangelical Church and The Church of the United Brethren in Christ.

The Church of The United Brethren in Christ traced its roots to a movement led by Philip William Otterbein (1726-1813). Otterbein came to America from Germany in 1752 as a minister of the Reformed Church. In 1754, after preaching a sermon on God's grace, Otterbein went to a guest room for private prayer. There he had an experience in which he found the inner assurance of God's love.

Approximately two years later, Otterbein went to a "great meeting" that had been called by Martin Boehm, a Mennonite preacher.

As Otterbein heard Boehm preach he became aware of the similar religious struggles and experiences they shared. After Boehm's sermon, Otterbein embraced him and declared in German, *"Wir sind Brüder!"* (We are brethren!)

The enthusiastic preaching of the two led to a movement that became The Church of The United Brethren in Christ. The new denomination consciously patterned itself after The Methodist Church in spirit and organization, but was largely for German-speaking people.

Otterbein was a friend of Frances Asbury and participated, at Asbury's request, in Asbury's ordination at the 1784 Christmas Conference — an early harbinger of our 1968 union.

The Evangelical Church traced its roots to Jacob Albright (1759-1808), a German-speaking Pennsylvanian who was a drummer in the Pennsylvania Militia during the American Revolution. He was affiliated with the Lutheran Church.

In 1790, several of Albright's children died in an epidemic, causing him to question the adequacy of his religious life. In his spiritual struggle, he sought the help of three men:

Anthony Houtz, a German Reformed minister who had conducted the children's funerals;

Isaac Davies, a Methodist lay preacher and neighborhood farmer;

Adam Riegel, another neighbor and an associate of Otterbein and Boehm.

For a time Albright affiliated with a Methodist class and held an exhorter's license, but he found it easier to communicate in German than in English, a preference which was reflected in the movement he led. Eventually the movement became the Evangelical Association, but it was sometimes referred to as the German Methodist Church.

Our Rich Ethnic Heritage

The United Methodist Church is an inclusive church whose heritage is not limited to its English and German roots, but is enriched by many races and cultures. In fact...

If all African American United Methodists were together in a separate denomination, it would be the seventh largest African American denomination in the nation.

If all Hispanic American United Methodists were together, it would be the second largest Spanish-speaking denomination in the country.

If all Native American United Methodists were together, it would be the largest Native American denomination.

If all Asian American United Methodists were together, it would be the largest Asian-American denomination in the nation.

But best of all, these Christians are *not* in separate denominations. They are a vital part of the beautiful rainbow of diversity that is The United Methodist Church!

Black Americans were present at the Christmas Conference in 1784:

> Harry Hosier, born a slave, became one of the favorite preachers and circuit riders of early American Methodism.

> Richard Allen was later to be named the first bishop of the African Methodist Episcopal Church.

Today all ethnic minority groups bring distinctive and valued gifts to our whole church. Some bring new hymns and new forms of worship. Some share an evangelistic zeal and a passionate commitment to social justice. Some teach us to be quiet, to be open and receptive to the Holy Spirit's work. All help us learn to live as Christians in an intercultural world.

If Otterbein were alive today, surely he would say, "We are brothers and sisters!"

Our Wider Methodist Family

The United Methodist Church is but one part of a world-wide fellowship of "the people called Methodist." With millions of other Christians we share common Wesleyan roots, very similar beliefs, and a joint commitment to Christ's mission in the world. In the United States, for example, we work with three sister denominations composed largely of Black Methodists:

The African Methodist Episcopal (AME) Church

The African Methodist Episcopal Zion (AME Zion) Church

The Christian Methodist Episcopal (CME) Church

Today our Methodist family encircles the globe. The United Methodist Church is one of sixty-three member churches in a world-wide association called The World Methodist Council. With some 24 million members, these Wesleyan denominations worship and work in ninety countries: Brazil... Estonia... Ghana... Mexico... New Zealand... Tonga... Uruguay... Zimbabwe... and many more.

BELIEFS

The United Methodist Church sails upon currents of belief arising in Judaism, modified by Jesus and the early church, and reformed by faithful Christians through the ages. Even in our own time the beliefs of the church are alive and moving, and each of us helps express them in new ways.

From Judaism

From the living Old Testament faith of Judaism, United Methodists have inherited an understanding of . . .

God as Creator of the world — a world that is good because God created it;

Our responsibility to care for the world God has entrusted to our keeping;

God as acting through human history;

and . . .

17

A special covenant relationship offered by God to a community of people;

God who is almighty and all-powerful, and yet who cares for us as a loving parent;

God as author of justice, who calls us to speak and work for justice as fearlessly as did Old Testament prophets;

God who both judges and offers mercy.

From the Early Church

With the New Testament church, we . . .

See that in Jesus Christ God is made known in the fullest way possible — in the flesh as a human being;

Accept the wholeness that God's forgiveness can restore — a forgiveness made concrete in the life and death of Jesus;

Celebrate the resurrection of Jesus Christ as the affirmation that God reigns over death as well as life;

Proclaim — in the sanctuary and throughout the world — that Jesus Christ is Lord!

From the Later Centuries

With the universal (catholic) church that spread across the Eastern and Roman Empires from the first century onward, United Methodists . . .

Affirm belief in the triune God — Father, Son, and Holy Spirit (the Creator, Redeemer, and Sustainer);

Recognize that rituals, symbols, and creeds can give faith expression;

Call for the fullest use of human reason to express our Christian faith —

— within a variety of cultures,
— in times of change,
— in light of new knowledge,
— to each new generation;

Understand that our faith can be given direction and our discipleship expressed within the world church and its organization.

From the Reformation

Our United Methodist beliefs reflect the major affirmations of Martin Luther, John Calvin, and other voices of the Protestant Reformation:

Salvation—a new and restored relationship to God—comes through our responding in faith to God's grace, to God's loving, free offer of such a relationship.

Faith is the placing of our complete trust in God.

Scripture is the primary source and guideline for doctrine. Each Christian has the opportunity—and responsibility—to read the Bible. We read it as members of the Christian fellowship even when we study alone.

The church is a "priesthood of all believers." Its members need no intermediary for communion with God, and they are in ministry with one another.

Proclamation of God's Word through preaching is a central part of worship.

From the Church of England

In England the principles of the sixteenth century Reformation were partially embodied in the new Church of England. Two centuries later John Wesley was an ordained minister of this Anglican Church, intent on reforming it further, but a faithful participant all his life.

From the Church of England we have inherited...

A recognition that the church's theology and decisions must be soundly based upon scripture, tradition, and reason;

An emphasis upon dignity and order in worship, as compared with more enthusiastic and informal styles of celebration.

A stress on the two sacraments affirmed by most Protestants — Baptism and Holy Communion.

Distinctive Emphases of United Methodists

We have inherited our central beliefs from Christians who have gone before us. But as United Methodists we also contribute our own emphases to Christian theology:

We respect diversity in theology. As long as our differences in belief are rooted in the essentials of the Christian faith, then these differences will enhance our understanding of God and challenge us to grow in faith.

We rely on God's grace for our salvation — grace that brings us to faith, grace that forgives us our sin and renews us, grace that continues to nurture us and draws us on toward perfect love.

We know that conversion and a new birth in Christ, whether sudden or gradual, occur under the guidance of the Holy Spirit.

We believe that faith in Christ is bound to be expressed in outward works of love — that personal salvation leads us into a mission of evangelical witness, caring service, and social action for human liberation, reconciliation, justice, and peace.

Our Theological Task

United Methodists believe that we are all theologians. God calls us to clarify and communicate our faith—to put our beliefs into words—for ourselves and for others. We do this using four sources or guidelines recommended by John Wesley:

Scripture—inspired by the Holy Spirit when it was written and *when it is read;* we are also aided by the research of biblical scholarship.

The church's tradition—the ever-renewed understandings of the faith community down through the ages.

Christian experience—the church's *and our personal* experience of God's healing love, the gift of new life in Christ.

Our reason—our capacity to analyze, compare, and come to sound judgments.

"These four sources—each making distinctive contributions, yet all finally working together—guide our quest as United Methodists for a vital and appropriate Christian witness" (from *The Book of Discipline—2004,* ¶104, page 83). We are invited—and called—to use these guidelines in making decisions in our lives and in the world.

MISSION

The United Methodist Church sees itself as part of a larger Christian fleet. Each ship—each denomination—has unique gifts that enable it to fulfill its special calling. Each has an understanding of its mission that contributes to the mission of the others.

The United Methodist Church has declared the primary task of its mission: *to make disciples for Jesus Christ.* The broader vision of that mission, however, is the mission Jesus proclaimed as his own when reading to his home synagogue in Nazareth:

> The Spirit of the Lord is upon me,
>   because he has anointed me
>   to bring good news to the poor.
> He has sent me to proclaim release to
>   the captives
>   and recovery of sight to the blind,
>   to let the oppressed go free....
>   (Luke 4:18-19)

We voice our own response and commitment as Christ's disciples in the vows we all take when becoming professing members of the church. These vows include a reaffirmation of the vows taken at baptism, by us or on our behalf: confession of Jesus Christ as Lord, acceptance and profession of the Christian faith as contained in the Old and New Testaments, and the promise to live a Christian life and remain a faithful member of Christ's holy church. Finally the vows include a specifically United Methodist question:

"Will you be loyal to The United Methodist Church, and uphold it by
    your prayers,
      your presence,
        your gifts, and
          your service?"

How do we live out—and how do we help others live out—these vows as disciples?

Our Prayers

We support the church's mission and ministry by our prayers in a variety of times and places:

When we are united in worship or fellowship with other members of the church;

When individually we pause spontaneously for prayer or turn to God during disciplined periods of meditation;

When, in our homes or other small groups, we hold up before God the members of our church, its leaders, its mission.

The church is strengthened when we . . .

Give thanks for what it means to us;

Confess its weakness, its needs;

Seek the renewing spirit of God in its life and work;

Commit ourselves to faithful membership and loving service.

We support the church by our prayers when we pray in the spirit of Jesus: "Thy kingdom come, thy will be done."

Our Presence

We fulfill our vows and are sustained—
when we are fully present *in body, mind, and
spirit* as our congregation gathers...

For regular worship in praise of God and
renewal of our lives;

For observance of the sacrament of Holy
Communion, which links us with that
first Lord's Supper and with other Christians throughout the centuries and
around the world;

For participation in the sacrament of Baptism, when we pledge to support those
being baptized — infants, youth, or adults
— in their growth in the faith;

For study, when we learn how our biblical
heritage speaks to our times and how our
faith calls us to live today.

We support the church by our presence
when we are fully present to one another in
times of need, hurt, and crisis — and in times
of rejoicing, fellowship, and thanksgiving.

Our Gifts

As God's children we have received many gifts — time, talent, energy, friends and family, a world of beauty and resources. But, as Jesus reminded us, we are not "owners" of these gifts, but "stewards."

Good stewards gratefully receive God's gifts, use them wisely, and share them liberally — not just because they "ought" to, but because of the joy and love in their faith. In part, we do this through the church. We support the church's mission through our gifts of leadership, service, and money.

We declare—and even sing:

> All things come of thee, O Lord; and
> of thine own have we given thee.
> (1 Chronicles 29: 14b and No. 588 in
> *The United Methodist Hymnal*)

Our Service

Jesus Christ came into the world "not to be served but to serve" (Mark 10:45). So we, as Christ's disciples, are called to be servants in the world that God loves.

> This ministry of all Christians in Christ's name and spirit is both a gift and a task. The gift is God's unmerited grace; the task is unstinting service. ... Entrance into and acceptance of ministry begin in a local church, but the impulse to minister always moves one beyond the congregation toward the whole human community.
> (*The Book of Discipline—2004,* ¶127).

Our service takes as many forms as there are needs. Our ministry is with persons near and far, young and old, rich and poor, whether Christian or not. It is a ministry with individuals, with groups, with institutions, with large social forces.

Most of our service is carried out through four large areas of responsibility:

Evangelism	Social concerns
Education	Worldwide mission

Let's look at each.

Our service is, in part, *evangelism.* Every United Methodist is called to be an evangelist —

To reach out to the troubled, the lonely, the apathetic — all those who feel cut off from the love of God and others;

To share with them the good news that the God of all loves them, that through faith in Jesus Christ a new life is possible;

To draw them into Christian fellowship and invite them to commit their lives to God as members of Christ's church;

To nurture them in the caring community, helping them to mature in faith and discipleship.

As evangelists, we respond to the risen Christ's "Great Commission":

"Go therefore and make disciples of all nations, baptizing them in the name of the Father, and of the Son and of the Holy Spirit, and teaching them to obey everything that I have commanded you. And remember, I am with you always, to the end of the age" (Matt. 28: 19-20).

Our service is, in part, a ministry of *teaching and learning*. As a church, through Christian education, we help persons...

Understand and use the Bible;

Understand and appreciate the church's history;

Discover the ways in which we are to live and serve as God's children;

Recognize that whatever lies beyond the horizon—although unknown and unseen—is in God's hands and is therefore good.

We recognize that educational ministry goes *beyond information*. It offers *transformation*.

As we take part in that transformation ministry, we find that we are both *life-long learners* (growing in Christian faith and discipleship) AND *life-long teachers* (helping others grow in faith and discipleship).

From our earliest Methodist beginnings we have found ways to express our faith through Christian education. To mention just a few examples:

The early Sunday school established in 1769 by Hannah Ball, a member of the Methodist Society at High Wycombe, England;

The summer assembly developed in the nineteenth century by Bishop John Vincent at Lake Chautauqua, New York, for the purpose of training Sunday school teachers;

Today's educational ministries in thousands of congregations with millions of children, youth, and adults learning the gospel and caring for one another in Sunday schools and other educational opportunities;

Nearly 120 United Methodist institutions of higher education — junior colleges, colleges, universities, and seminaries — all affirmations of our commitment to develop the mind as a gift from God.

In part our service is our informed and active response to *social concerns.* Individually, in groups, as congregations, and with other churches and agencies, we work . . .

To assure justice for those who may have no other voice;

To create avenues of communication to replace barriers of distrust and prejudice among persons, institutions, and nations;

To enable and encourage Christians to express their convictions in the decision-making arenas of politics and public policy;

To awaken persons to their responsibilities to care for the creation—including the human body—that has been entrusted to us.

Our United Methodist position on social issues is examined and redefined every four years by the General Conference. These "Social Principles" cover a wide sweep of concerns: the natural world, the nurturing community (for example, families), and social, economic, political, and world community issues.

Lastly, to be in service is to take up our part in the *worldwide mission* of the church. In a sense, we are all missionaries. Through study, financial support, prayer, and direct participation, we carry on Christ's mission in all states, all nations, all continents—in every place where people are in need.

We offer medical services to persons who would otherwise suffer and die;

We feed those who would otherwise starve, and provide technical know-how that will help persons produce their own food better;

We educate persons so they can realize their own worth and improve the conditions in which they live;

We join others in awareness that we are members of one global family, that what affects one affects the others;

We proclaim—in both word and deed— that God's Word has become flesh in the midst of God's world.

ORGANIZATION

The organization through which The United Methodist Church carries out its work might be compared to the elaborate system of masts, sails, and rigging on a large sailing ship. When skillfully trimmed to respond to the inspiration ("the breath") of God, the ship can sail magnificently and on course with full sails into the wind. If, however, the sails exist only for the convenience of the crew or just to make the ship look good, then the ship can falter off course and wander in meaningless circles.

Let's briefly examine the major organizational structures that guide The United Methodist Church:

Local Church

District

Annual Conference

Jurisdictional Conference (in the U.S.)

Central Conference (outside the U.S.)

General Conference

The Local Church

To be a United Methodist is to be part of a specific congregation linked to more than 35,000 other congregations in the United States and nearly 8,000 in other countries.

The local church is a community of "persons who have been baptized, have professed their faith in Christ, and have assumed the vows of membership in The United Methodist Church" (from *The Book of Discipline—2004,* ¶203). Members are strengthened and sustained in their faith and life through fellowship, hearing the Word of God, and receiving the sacraments—in order that they may minister to persons both within and outside the church.

Lay members are assisted in their ministry by *ordained ministers,* appointed annually by the bishop. Those ordained as *elders* proclaim and teach the word, administer the sacraments, offer pastoral guidance, and provide administrative leadership.

Those ordained as *deacons* lead members in relating congregational life and worship with service to God in the world; they may lead members through such specialized areas as education and music.

Each congregation must have certain *basic* organizational units, but it also can form units to best serve its situation and ministries. The *basic units*:

The *Charge Conference* meets annually to (1) connect the local church and the general church, (2) evaluate the total ministry of the church, (3) adopt objectives and goals for ministry, and (4) elect the leaders who will help fulfill these objectives and goals.

The *Church Council* meets at least quarterly to provide for planning and implementation of programs and ministries of *nurture, outreach,* and *witness.* At least annually the council plans for the congregation's future ministry and mission. In some congregations the council may be called the *Administrative Board.*

The *Committee on Lay Leadership,* known before 2001 as the Committee on Nominations and Personnel, (1) coordinates the church leadership needs and (2) nominates key officers for election by the Charge Conference.

The *Committee on Pastor-Parish or Staff-Parish Relations* (1) counsels with and supports the employed staff of the church, (2) evaluates their work, and (3) cooperates with the district superintendent and bishop in the appointment of ordained ministers or a local pastor to the church.

The *Trustees* oversee the church property concerns and legal matters.

The *Committee on Finance* manages the church's money concerns, including the development of an annual budget and its recommendations to the Church Council.

Ministries of nurture, outreach, and mission can be implemented in a variety of ways. The organization should be determined by the congregation's resources, challenges, and faithfulness in responding to God's call.

Through the *nurturing ministries*, the church addresses its concerns for and commitment to *education, worship*, and *stewardship*. A congregation may have one *ministry team* (or commission or work area, for example) responsible for education, one for worship, and one for stewardship. Another congregation may have one ministry unit for all three. While another may develop its own unique combination of ministry units. (The same organizing options apply, of course, to outreach and witness ministries as discussed below.)

Through its *outreach ministries*, the church responds to local and global issues of justice and compassion.

Through *witness ministries* the church attends to evangelistic outreach, membership care, and spiritual formation.

Ordained ministers serve as members of units related to their responsibilities. A *lay leader* elected by the Charge Conference is a member of several of these bodies who serves to interpret opportunities for lay ministry. And one or more *lay member(s) of the annual conference* link(s) the Charge Conference and Church Council with the annual conference.

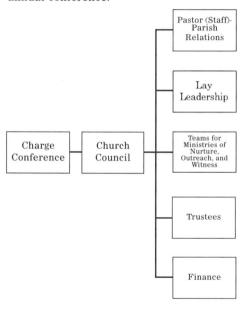

Teams for nurture, outreach, and witness ministries may be as streamlined or as detailed as needs and resources suggest.

The District

Local churches may be grouped together in various ways: circuits, cooperative parishes, clusters, subdistricts. But *every* church in the U. S. A. is part of a *District* of some thirty to ninety congregations.

The District is a division of the Annual Conference and serves as a link between the local church and the conference. Each District is led by a district superintendent, an ordained minister appointed by the bishop, usually for a six-year term. He or she . . .

Relates each congregation to the wider structures of the church;

Serves as a pastor to the clergy and their families;

Sees that the churches of the District function as required by *The Book of Discipline;*

Presides over the Charge Conference meetings;

Coordinates the work of the District through the District Council on Ministries and other District structures.

The Annual Conference

The term *Annual Conference* is used by United Methodists in the United States in several ways: It is an organizational structure, a geographical area, and a periodic meeting of persons (usually then called an "Annual Conference session").

The Annual Conference is made up of clergy members, active and retired, and (in equal numbers) lay members elected by each Charge Conference. It meets . . .

To worship and fellowship as the church;

To receive reports, adopt goals and programs, and determine budgets for carrying out the church's mission;

To take stands on key issues reflecting the church's witness to society;

To receive new men and women into the ordained and diaconal ministry;

To elect delegates to Jurisdictional and General Conferences (every four years);

To receive the bishop's appointments of ordained ministers.

The bishop of the *episcopal area* (which may include more than one Annual Conference) presides over the Annual Conference session and serves as general superintendent of the churches in the conference. He or she is assisted by the cabinet (the district superintendents of the annual conference).

The Jurisdiction

The United Methodist Church in the U.S.A. is divided into five areas known as *Jurisdictions:* Northeastern, Southeastern, North Central, South Central, and Western. Jurisdictions provide some programs and leadership training events to support annual conference work. Every four years, the Jurisdictional Conferences meet to elect new bishops and select members of general boards and agencies.

The Central Conference

In addition to the Annual Conferences in the United States, there are several *Central Conferences* in other parts of the world: Africa, Europe, and the Philippines. They are a full part of The United Methodist Church, with their own bishops and their own delegates to General Conference.

The General Conference
and Church Agencies

The only body with authority to speak officially for The United Methodist Church is the *General Conference.* Made up of an equal number of lay and clergy delegates elected by the Annual and Central Conferences, it meets every four years to conduct the business of the church.

The General Conference has the power to make and change the laws governing the church, to revise *The Book of Discipline,* to establish program emphases for the quadrennium, and authorize the four-year budget for the church's general work.

The *Council of Bishops* provides guidance and oversight between General Conference sessions. The *Judicial Council* serves as the "Supreme Court" of the church, ruling upon the constitutionality of actions of General Conference and other bodies and officers of the church.

The *General Council on Finance and Administration* acts as treasurer to the church as a whole.

In addition there is a *Connectional Table* which brings together representatives of the general agencies to coordinate efforts and promote cooperation.

There are also *general boards* and other *commissions* and *agencies:*

General Board of Church and Society
General Board of Discipleship
General Board of Global Ministries
General Board of Higher Education and Ministry
General Board of Pension and Health Benefits
General Commission on Archives and History
General Commission on Communication (United Methodist Communications)
General Commission on Christian Unity and Interreligious Concerns
General Commission on Religion and Race
General Commission on the Status and Role of Women
General Commission on United Methodist Men
The United Methodist Publishing House

At all levels our organization exists only to help the church fulfill Christ's mission. In the end we place our organizational structures—as well as our lives—in God's hands to be reformed and renewed for this mission.

FOR FURTHER READING

These resources will guide your further exploration of United Methodist history, beliefs, mission, and organization. Items published by Discipleship Resources may be ordered online at www.discipleshipresources.org; by phone at 800-972-0433; by fax at 615-340-7590; or by mail from Customer Services, PO Box 340012, Nashville, TN 37203-0012. (Resources from other publishers are available from Cokesbury.)

The Book of Discipline of The United Methodist Church (United Methodist Publishing House). Updated every four years.

Evangelism and Theology in the Wesleyan Spirit, by Albert C. Outler (Discipleship Resources, 1996). The late Dr. Outler's keen theological insight and deep commitment provide rewarding reading for those seeking a deeper understanding of their heritage and faith.

The History of The Evangelical United Brethren Church, by J. Bruce Behney and Paul H. Eller (Abingdon Press, 1979). A thorough presentation of the movements that led to the formation of The Evangelical United Brethren Church and its 1968 union with The Methodist Church.

Living Our Beliefs, by Kenneth L. Carder (Discipleship Resources, 1996). Bishop Carder invites thoughtful reflection on and response to a tradition that insists true beliefs must be *lived.*

The Organization of the United Methodist Church, 2002 Edition, by Jack M. Tuell (Abingdon Press, 2002). Bishop Tuell provides helpful insight in understanding the organization of the denomination.

Our Membership Vows in The United Methodist Church, by Mark W. Stamm (Discipleship Resources, 2002). Examines the meaning of the vows in our baptismal covenant.

The United Methodist Primer, 2001 Revised Edition, by Chester E. Custer (Discipleship Resources, 2001). Chet Custer invites us to consider our faith as a journey, recognizing our rich heritage and beliefs, challenging us to understand and act.

What Every Leader Needs to Know About United Methodist Connections, by Linda R. Whited (Discipleship Resources, 2004). One of a series designed to help lay and clergy leaders in the local church.

What Every Teacher Needs to Know About The United Methodist Church (Discipleship Resources, 2002). One of a series designed to provide Christian educators with knowledge necessary for effective teaching.